Mortalia

James Owens

FUTURECYCLE PRESS

www.futurecycle.org

Published by FutureCycle Press
Lexington, Kentucky, USA

ISBN 978-1-942371-12-0

for erin wilson

Contents

RED THOUGHT WITHIN A GLADIOLUS BLOSSOM

—after a photograph by erin wilson

The image is a garden inside the garden.

Eros as shimmer
as blood unfurls
through the wall of this wound
that opens the air like a sex.

The strokes of her looking
breathe
the petals to further opening and opening
and un-
fold
membrane contour texture.
Different wet reds shine.

All this from dirt and sun and water
dust the flower has healed
sepal
ovule
anthers laden dark
nudge of a cell upward
any touch would soft to bursting
and scatter sperm
inside the four chambers of the stone.

Frotteur

1.

Like a vast neural
   diagram, the same
   branch
and twig shadows as usual

waver beneath the winter trees,
   washed and dim
   this morning
when clouds veil the sun,

indistinct, gauzy,
   floating a
   centimeter
above the surface,

but when the wind draws the clouds back,
   the sun comes fulgent,
   weighting
the trees, and tightens

the shadows against snow,
   hardens them from gray
   to black,
flexing a muscle in the color,

the resonant solidity
   that darkens dense bodies
   in winter:
crows, thistle stalks, fence posts.

2.

But when I say "flexing a muscle,"
    I think,
    without thinking,
of the sweet, slick clench

of your cunt, that first day
    we made love,
    and how,
as you neared coming,

something like accusation
    clouded your face,
    or dread
for the wrenching that takes a body,

and when I kissed the smooth skin
    just under your navel,
    a muscle
there still fluttered,

as if in surprise.
    The spirit,
    whatever
and wherever that is,

studies the sun, and here
    the body,
    its shadow,
darkens, thickens, is.

3.

The summer when I had lost
 the first world and
 was void,
I ached for skin on skin,

for something to pierce
 the leathery, desperate
 sheath,
so I would, sick with lack,

secretly, recklessly, uselessly
 touch the strayed wisps
 of women's hair
in line at the grocery store—

and once, just once,
 leaving a movie, I discovered
 a tall,
angular girl ahead in the crowd

and maneuvered
 until my bare forearm
 brushed
her bare forearm in the hurrying past.

I glanced aside, as if
 the contact were
 accidental,
while the pure charge of presence leapt

alive through my forlorn skin,
 salvation in the weight
 of joint and bone,
restored, pressing the earth.

Letter to Erin from a Winter Dawn in Indiana

The snowy fields ache, hollow with want.
I shake before the photograph of your breasts

and understand the fox we saw, no fluff-tailed trickster,
scrawny and tattered, muscles like twists of wire

bunched under his summer-cheapened pelt,
a killer. Need shapes me now,

and it is right for scarcity to whet the fat away,
to find the hooks of bone and tendon.

It was also good to gorge and fatten
to surfeit and past—I mean our marriage bed

where bodies fed body and spirit, hour on hour,
until our skins grew sleek on each other's heat.

Here I don't rest.
Distance and weeks of hunger for you

harrow me as that fox knew famine. Remember
his thighs, coiled, stalking, and in the perfect arc of desire

he pounced on the field mouse in the roadside grass,
tearing after meat, his jaws working?

I warn you, it is that kind of need.
I am returning merciless and starved.

WOMAN AND BEAR

An ordinary day. Enough sunlight to sketch pale shadows

on the fallen leaves. I would like to say this light is filmy
and sleek, like some undergarment tossed aside in a hurry,

puddled silk on the floor of the sky—but it isn't.
I am only wishing for you. Across the street,

the council of starlings debates hunger in a broad maple.
Somewhere colder, the bear you met by the river tears apart a log

for a meal of white grubs, plunging claws in the soft wood,
fattening himself, as winter begins to glow around his heart.

The bear is real. The querulous note when you told me
of woman and hump-shouldered, hungry bear

staring at each other across the water—
if not for the pain, you said, *what a glorious death.*

That same slant music quavers in the shadows
when a cloud passes. If we must die, and we must,

why not silted into the warm fat of a wintering bear?

How easily you could have slipped from this world.
Hearing, I wanted to lift your hips to me like a wooden bowl.

Do you see how knowing your transience
makes this a love poem? At once, for no reason,

the whole flock of starlings glitters, unfurls from the tree,
reels squabbling twice around the yard, and settles back.

The Edge of the Ice

Cold binds pale breath to the earth.
Alone, I don't speak, to save heat,

or I speak because my distant mouth needs it.
The world cracks underfoot.

My hands remember refuge,
the warmth beneath her breasts.

She said, *if there were only one landscape,*
it should be gray with a single red berry at the center.

Neither Speech nor Silence

I will love you then by saying your death.
Is this a gift, your death
a failing gesture in the voice?
Awake in the early still-dark,
I will beat hollow a grave
inside my breathing to bury
your death, the frantic muteness,
the hallowed word your name
to come to void here,
a finish. No other rest then,
I will be like those cursed
who flee when none pursues.
The black draft your death
will be is already my aphasia.
I can barely speak this now—
then you will break the wires
between words and their
referents. This blankness
is the cost of touching your
death: *tree river stone*
love body light, meaning impossible,
forever a gasping toward
a no, no room to shape
the air into a denial, no shape,
words fraying from the mouth,
no space for them to travel through.

Before Spring

Then, later in the afternoon, after crossing the white fields,
we step together over a berm of snow beside the common road
where wind gleams in the sinuosities of tall winter grass.

Daylight clings close and deepens the marrow
of the landscape, even as shadows bulk out from the pines.
The tufts of sinewy, thin blades rub and delay the shine,

exactly as the fibrous sheaf of the body defers the spirit's passage
back to the earth, exactly so, to slow its arrival,
or, if there is no spirit, to clutch fire in the tangled atoms

for a moment longer, before they slack apart and fall again
through the void. Already we lean toward evening.
We touch the rustling stems as roughly as the wind,

knowing soon we will hurry home to uncover skin,
to offer warmth like sweetness near the bone—*here,*
where I kneel before the tender gate of my lover's womb.

Salmon Run, Kagawong, Ontario, 2013

1.

We decided not to have a child
and now walk together beside this teeming.
Cold pries flushed leaves from the maples
above water heaving with flesh.
I want my wife's breasts. She undoes a button
and folds my hands into the warmth under her clothes,
and I waver near regret, never knowing if the choice
was wisdom or cowardice, unwilling to risk chaos,
unwilling to pay the time—our melancholy,
grown-up caution before the violence of desire.
But I touch her and tell myself I know our child,
curled hank of vein and bone swimming through her
that would have knotted
our temporary blood to this falling and surge.

2.

I have never seen this before:
the traveled fish thrash uphill,
stubborn as hammered spikes,

hovering to rest
in the lucid pools, then bursting out,
tails beating the ice water

over ruffling shoals,
urgent toward reproduction
and death. When one loses

its grip on the water, the current
sweeps it far back until it catches
somehow and climbs again,

a thick, single-minded
sleeve of flesh pulsing
like a horse's thigh muscle.

The untiring, convulsive salmon
whip themselves above
the slick, algae-green stones,

against the also stubborn
invisible current, yellow-
black ripples of shimmer and

thrust—or, each a fist
clenched on roe or milt,
they punch a tunnel through water

to quiet where they will gasp
and drop their milky heat
into the dangerous chill of this world.

NEURAESTHETIC

The brain shapes itself to clutch memory. For example,
I have never seen columbine along this stream before,

but here they are, red blossoms in the shade on the bank,
small folded lanterns nodding in a curt breeze, as water

swift with the slope of its bed ruffles and gurgles
toward Lake Huron, a cool suffused clarity over rocks

bronzed in the June sunlight and green-striated with streamers
of moss waving in the flow, as the flowers wave above in the air,

and in response my brain restructures a fine thread of protein,
a wisp of me as sleek as the chalaza curdled in egg white, and this

is a memory. It is physical, an electrically excitable,
unique chemical sequence that means these columbines'

thin stems and the corners of blooms like the bent legs of insects,
this color of petals, red just emerging wet from a sugary pink,

clustered around a yellow interior velvety with sex organs.
And a neuronal aesthetics is born—beyond noting the bare fact

that columbines grow here to *what it is like* to know them—
in this memory's cross-linking with other encoded wisps,

a mesh that gleams with specifics, the shine of slick-washed stones
under the tumbling water, an aspen shivering, birds, the fungal smell

of dirt licked away where the bank has caved beneath a mat of roots,
though the linkages also extend through time to the autumn day

when Erin and I breathed cold here and watched golden-sided salmon
punch tunnels through the current, and to another day another summer

when I sat reading Miroslav Holub and sweating, over-dressed
against mosquitoes thick as pepper in the air, but stubborn to be here.

Why? Why such complexity and over-indexing in memory,
the simple, reportable fact, useful to the tribe, woven this deeply

into the web of sense impressions and association, smell and color
and taste of a never-repeated breeze, the warmth of particular skin?

Is it because the aesthetic makes the fact richer, more likely
to be recalled and told and attended? Or is it because

I find myself imaged in this, where the ramifying signal-flicker
ghosting in gel beneath an arch of bone seems a compensatory mirror

for the world always slipping over its horizon, already lost,
but weighted, real, incarnate still in the arbitrary detail?

A bit further along the trail, a wooden footbridge crosses the creek,
a few meters upstream from a fallen pine whose branches

break and braid the fast water to icy lace, and the plank handrail
is littered with maple samaras, and lovers must have passed here,

strangers, traces scored in boxy, knife-point carving:

DEVLAND

CHARLENE

SENSE

In the end, there is nothing
to say, except gratitude

for the articulation of muscle
and skin, solidity of bone,

and the fine webbing of nerve
that nets consciousness

and coddles it here in the senses,
fired tangle and delay.

In the thin, almost infinite gaps
between neurons, we discover

together that the body
is deferral, is weight and wait,

ballast and balance
that slows the spirit,

keeps everything from flashing
to crisis at the one,

sudden flowering of ache.

Otherwise, it would not matter
that my fingertips

start just under your ear
and move with impossible

luxury, almost undetectable touch,
down the side of the breathing

throat, over the collarbone
and the supreme smooth paleness

of the shoulder,
down the inside of your arm,

finding the slight blue veins
of the wrist, and lingering

long in the palm.
Without the body,

why would I want
the gesture to consume a thousand years?

Without the body, where
would memory knot

us to the world?
Once we stood on a rim of granite

above a northern lake, and upward
through the bare birch

and tamarack, hoof beats rose
into the same cold air we breathed.

A body larger than both of us
was alive there.

Now we say nothing, but memory
in your white breast

answers and stirs, stiffens
to meet memory in my warm mouth.

Letter to Erin from Gore Bay at the End of August

The compact silence of stones when shadows
of beach grass flicker across them in the wind—

if I note these things, will they weigh
more real for you, or for a longer time?

A small boat on the water, and someone wears a red shirt.
When wind comes in from the lake,

voices blow toward me, a gruff stumble of
drunken singing, at ease, I think, in the lightly

floating pod of a self, and a quieter voice,
steadily urging some caution that I can't make out.

Which speaker wears red? Small waves
shush and retreat, a milky sheen on their backs,

opal more than milk, as the late sun slants low,
honed edges folding into themselves.

I have waded out past the slippery rocks
and swam with gulls floating nearby—

now I listen by the waves, shirtless, beginning
to shiver in the first late-summer chill,

glad for the blanket around my shoulders,
the promise of warm sleep rising in me like water,

and soon a drive in darkness from this island
back to you, lifting sheets to lie by your body.

Twilight thickens to hide the mind that desires these things,
as if we began at dawn by remembering the relinquished earth,

and I have landed here, finally,
to watch it disassemble again

and tatter down around me, as always on such evenings.
We desire that the world endure, last,

knowing in advance that all will be lost,
but leaning to the voices from the drifting boat,

wanting the gull pecking at the edge of the water,
the black cormorant tacking farther from shore,

the earthy smell of weed cover that could almost
be sweetgrass but is not.

MIGRATION

The day comes, perhaps in your fiftieth year,
when you know the rest of it is a letting go.
Parents will die and soon. Children, grown
long and angular, will choose strangers and leave.
The shadows of branches will fall through the space
you knotted into a body, and the sunlight
that warms your cheek like a hand is not a hand.
The future is velocity and Impressionist smears
of color, snow and frozen earth, blood—
this ordinary knowledge is as still
and lethal as water in a boarded-over well,
and no words will make it better or worse.
After that, you will drive the backroad fence-lines,
when rain has smudged twilight onto maple leaves,
and the wind of the coolest summer in memory
glances off the yellow and purple of ragweed and thistle
and smooths the lacy heads of young wheat
like copperish fur the fields lift to be smoothed.
Sandhill cranes will rise from a field left fallow,
thick with tall grass and groundsel and chicory,
almost rife enough to hide the birds, except for
the lithe necks and ruddy crowns bobbing and curious.
You stop to see. Three row heavily into the air
and level off, and you think that is all,
long, thin bodies laboring against their own density
to find the easy point where momentum
outbalances weight, but then four more rise
and a dozen more, as if birthed from wet farmland
that opens and shudders them toward the slate sky,
and twenty more, you beside the car now and shouting
astonishment up into their midst, one wordless word
lost in the slow, washboard rattle of their calls.
Then they are past, the improbable contrivances
of wing and feather disappearing in formation.
You stand a moment in the quiet and then go home.

Love Poem for This Morning's Raven
on the Leafless Walnut Branch

It is stunning enough that the world makes a raven,
incomprehensible that it makes this raven, with the broken

feather at the edge of its left wing,
the little gargling hitch halfway through its call.

Why caress the unique so hotly? The idea "raven"
may be necessary to complete the cosmos,

but why this bewildering specificity, each
raven a singular night-colored pivot for the sky,

each a black keyhole slit in the air, where we
fall through a raven's eyes and fade?

This is how we know the world is poetry, not philosophy.
If philosophy were the world, it would say "raven" once

and be still,
but since the world is poetry, it repeats

"this raven" infinitely, lingering, sensuous, over
the small particulars of plume and beak and sheen.

ECSTASIS

Rustle and gleam in the understory,
a breeze lifts the little lanterns of columbine,

lit scarlet like tongues by the fire
they lick up through marl and leaf-rot.

Lanterns. And tongues. Stamen
and tendril sieving the wind, an ache

for the right turn of air, for the word
that will burn the words away,

a spray of yellow pollen.

And the same shine everywhere—
on the segmented back of the five-inch

purple-black millipede on the path, pedaling
crazy bright panic as he arcs up

and over a fallen, wet twig of birch.

A Morning

A worm as thin as an *i* or a snipped thread,
of a synthetic green you would never know
was natural, the knot of its strange blood
a little gemstone ticking in its head,
risks death on the rim of my sleeve to knead
and softly knead its half-inch of earth.
This perfect being flung itself unfelt, unhurt
as a breath, from a birch leaf. It liked my heat
and curled up to wait through all the turns
of the dark, there where I hung my naked shirt,
because it believed without words
and without knowing it lacked the words
that every day that wakes some warmth returns.

SALAMANDER

Like a clutch of wet leaves
kicked up in the snow
on the path beside the swamp.
Ice frozen to its sides
he couldn't brush clean.
Eyes frozen to blind shards.
Trembling. He left it there,
but all day he feels
it dying, an amputation
hugged to his chest,
a sleeve in the wind,
soft with ghost pain.
This will happen to some of us.
A spark misfires
in the hibernating brain,
and you wake to the wrong season.
Born again from the nourishing,
amniotic mud, ready
to thrum with love
for the day—
you crawl into
a stunned world
of inconceivable white fire.

A Woman Photographing Turtle Eggs

She loves the clutch of shells, broken,
emptied, left. She lifts them
one by one in her palm

to weigh their weightlessness
against her breath, their touch
against her skin. She thinks

of the eggs inside the warm mother,
how each slid free at the right time
and shielded a life as it nudged

into being and particular shape,
tiled carapace and plastron
and claws and hooked mouth

all perfect in their solidity, fact
knitted from the egg's liquid.
The young, curled in each private

chamber of the sun-wombed nest,
breathed slowly through shell and dirt,
and perhaps, near hatching,

they sometimes heard footsteps,
faint news from the unguessed
air of light and menace and food,

though they were earth-held secrets
who had not yet suffered
the first of all thoughts: *come forth.*

Breathing Late in Winter

The season's news was bombs and numbers killed.
The river tied and untied itself, slipping
the grip of rocks and hiding one icy wing
under another then another, prolific and wild
as bird or angel, not fallen but felled
and rapt with attention to its own nothing—
the shifting yield of current and depth, in-folding
earthward, sky on its back sheer and rippled.
Snow gleamed. The little *I* walked past formal trees
that stiffened their veins against frigid air
and held life close, a wet thread through the core.
The nest of wire in the chest rang and breathed
a cold that burned blood from the lungs, that grieved
the mouth to silence like the gasp of distant war.

Just North, Spring Leans into a Valley
Like a Mennonite Woman Opening Her Dress

The difficult landscape
holds life close,
a wet persistent pulse
faint in frozen earth,
and still in late March

patches of snow soften
in thickets of pine shade.
A week ago was winter.
Swamps of broken ice
splintered the reborn sun,

but now yellow catkins
brighten birch twigs,
and the season's mad frogs
rub off their last chill
to shout and rut in muck.

This farm woman braced
her prayers against the weather,
suffered buffets of squall
and lake-heavy storms
burying acres of sky,

her face rough in wind,
hands hard as thorn
to the necessary work.
Now she unbuttons her blouse,
gathers her skirt above

her knees. She breathes,
offers nipples like tight
red buds, skin renewed
as the turned wheat field.
She shudders when she comes.

Swamp

The toxins silting down my blood would rest
in the deep-floored acres of mud and rot.
Here is everything's end—clenched stumps unknot
from softened ground, a floating log like a fist
on another log skins strips of pale bark.
Decay unknits the forgotten. A clotting mist
of spores and stench rises above weeds and darkens.
Reflected clouds fail. The sun does not exist.

I slack at roadside and wait for word
to something ill in me, some tidal urge to lie
and sink through mud to mud, all history blurred
and faltering, a sourceless will to die—
but here's no welcome, only the black, slurred
sloth of water, then a hawk's tall, clean cry.

From the Rocks Above Bass Pond

I bang fist-sized stones together. Once.
Stones cool with the smell of dirt
from lying in the ferns.
My palms love their gritty sides.

The hollow *tonk* plucks at air
like a first raindrop hitting a spider's web,
the shape of a word
whose only content is attention.

The solemn turkey buzzard shrugs higher.
Gray moss cracks underfoot.
Juniper and blueberry clench small.
Here, wind and weak sun;

below, the fur of trees ruffles,
and the pond glints,
losing track of my failures.
I would lie and wither like the moss

and rise in a year, language as hard
and unused as a scatter of pebbles,
to find my own crossed thighbones here,
stripped sticks to knock together for prayer.

Purple Sweetness at the Edge of Vision

There are more sparrows than you will ever name,
flitting brown and cliché from the edge of a thicket,
until they are invisible in their subtle variants,

until their songs are a gray lilt in the background
you would notice only if they stopped singing.
And don't mention insects, an inordinate fondness

for beetles played out like a parody of formal invention.
Mortality might begin with the thought
that culture is more interesting than nature.

Resurrection starts with the knowledge
that nature and culture become one.
Late September, and bumblebees grazing thistle bloom

tip themselves face-down in the purple sweetness,
kicking for balance, like ducks
nuzzling weeds in a creek's bottom ooze.

The comparison is not in the thistle, nor in the bees,
who know nothing of MacDiarmid's bloody-minded drunkard,
or of Tanizaki's *Some Prefer Thistles*.

But no, that's wrong, I realize—as we walk on, leaving the bees
to their luscious debauch—no, Tanizaki wrote about nettles,
and the sweet, ignorant bees would never confuse the two,

though we push through the mist of indistinguishable song,
the wrong names at our lips, insisting
all prickly weeds must be somehow the same.

Dandelion Is

not only the buttery froth of bloom,
strut and defiance and sex, pulse,
sap, heads one morning in the grass,
eager little sun-warm erections,

nor yet the gray spiritual
fluff clocks, sketching their skeletal
longing away from the earth,
that shiver toward the wind and go,

but the downward clot of root,
unkillable, fibrous, that sucks wet
from the dirt, breaks upward,
digs in like teeth and chews the stone.

Rise

It comes unsought—*only* unsought.

It comes uninvited—*only* uninvited—
and by preference at the core of sorrow,
when sorrow without relief

slumps into the mind like thick,
obvious mud: the sick child,
the fallen marriage, the failing

god who hides his fragments
in debris, weeks when you learn
sorrow is the only possibility.

It comes like this. One evening
you trudge along, broken,
a street chosen because choice

doesn't matter, watching your numb
shoes—and for no reason at all
the late-spring light lifts itself

up from the late-spring lawns,
and the two sullen teens,
glaring as you pass, move

toward each other's hands,
and the sun through thin cloud
has just enough day left

to burn the glass
of a stone church
free of its gray blur,

so that gold and blue now flash
and yearn, and the sky
trembles, ready.

From the Scripture of Reeds and Shallows

Hieratic, the heron paces the shallows
like a serious pastor with hands folded

against his spine, meditating the lessons
of small fish, the choreography of frogs,

and at my approach flaps from the water's edge,
a poor construct of scrap board and paper

rigged with wire and pulled slapdash
into the wind, fighting for a moment

the weight of earth, heft of body, but rising,
easing now into grace between the wings.

I ask him, disappearing, to pray for us
and turn, having tired of the wind.

TEMPLE

Leaves filter valuable scraps of sun, the same energy
that heaved ice from the ground two months ago

and now shivers out into birch catkins
littering the soil beneath the birches

after rain, like a carpet of fuzzy worms,
and maple samaras, just as thick,

rotoring down a rain of detached wings
when a breeze brushes them free.

Energy invents shape against contingent
fact, pushing out to warm the curves

and crenellated, given limits of a world
nor chance nor design. This is meaning: a lyric

flush of detail, crimping along
the lucent, veined edge of a maple key

that fills the cleared space of the mind,
understanding like music against late-spring chill

where the sun breathes an opening in the trees.

The Only Real Work Is to Become Grass

The wet brown air dreams of green, urging
stems through the rotting, matted sleep
of twigs and fungus and torn leaf,

where fronds press the ragged sides of fallen birches,
the open hands of small women, fringed
with veins like a tracery of fingerprints.

On my knees, I lift one to see the different
paler green of the underside and stroke
the secret join where thinner stems branch.

But I disappoint myself, soon bored
with beauty, and drift to the river,
gray under clouds. Tough, ordinary grass

blows and rustles beside the water.
Nondescript twigs cross and rub
on leafless bushes I can't identify.

The river keeps flowing past.
It is that kind of world. No metaphor,
here at some distance from the ferns—

the grass is grass, the twigs
are twigs, and crows in the distance
gloat over some death they have discovered.

(Death is essential. And the ferns
were not really dreaming, not really small hands,
those organic engines for burning leaf rot.)

I lie lost on my belly, watching grass,
the coolness of dirt seeping in,
the wind and water moving.

Grass will grow through my hands.

Albedo

The way north of town is rough with slush
and tire ruts, mud-slick in the hollows, slopes
washboard runnel, jounce and skid.
Late March, still a waist-deep berm
of plowed snow at the roadsides,
then knee-deep, crusted snow in the serious
bush after a week of thaw and freeze.

It is Sunday morning. Somebody pours prayer
on the ruined column of void we call our hearts.
Somebody strops the word *love* to a razor's gleam.
I park to walk a smaller, worse road,
and on the hills, stands of birch blur with distance
to drifts of gray smoke against a screen of pine.
Shadows of branches in slant sun
clutch at the snow's glare.

I go head down, dazzled half blind.
A week ago, we hiked a snow machine trail
a few miles from here, where a wolf crossed
from forest to forest, silent, close,
pausing just yards ahead to glance back,
his shadow edged and arched, starving for meat.

Today, dark water slides under a gap
in river ice. Crows slick
their opaque cries on the sky. White trunks
of birch tremble like a wife's thighs.
Back home in the afternoon,
Erin tells me she found a caterpillar

wakened early on asphalt and thought to save it
from the path of cars. It curled and uncurled,
furry on her palm, tender black face butting
her thumb—but only hard snow on both sides,
nowhere warm to lay the caterpillar down.
Nowhere, she says, a rent despair shaking her.

Acknowledgments

Boxcar Poetry Review: "Salamander"

Clinch Mountain Review: "Dandelion Is"

Connecticut River Poetry Review: "Just North, Spring Leans into a Valley Like a Mennonite Woman Opening her Dress"

The Cresset: "Ecstasis," "Rise"

Floodwall: "From the Rocks Above Bass Pond"

Flycatcher: "Woman and Bear"

Heron Tree: "Neither Speech nor Silence"

Kentucky Review: "Red Thought Within a Gladiolus Blossom"

One: "The Only Real Work Is to Become Grass"

Sow's Ear Poetry Review: "Purple Sweetness at the Edge of Vision"

Superstition Review: "Love Poem for This Morning's Raven on the Leafless Walnut Branch"

Town Creek Poetry: "From the Scripture of Reed and Shallow," "Letter to Erin from Gore Bay at the End of August"

Valparaiso Poetry Review: "Albedo," "Temple"

Cover photo, "Turtle Egg," and author photo by erin wilson; cover and interior book design by Diane Kistner; Charter text with Mate titling

About FutureCycle Press

FutureCycle Press is dedicated to publishing lasting English-language poetry books, chapbooks, and anthologies in both print-on-demand and ebook formats. Founded in 2007 by long-time independent editor/publishers and partners Diane Kistner and Robert S. King, the press incorporated as a nonprofit in 2012. A number of our editors are distinguished poets and writers in their own right, and we have been actively involved in the small press movement going back to the early seventies.

The FutureCycle Poetry Book Prize and honorarium is awarded annually for the best full-length volume of poetry we publish in a calendar year. Introduced in 2013, our Good Works projects are anthologies devoted to issues of universal significance, with all proceeds donated to a related worthy cause. Our Selected Poems series highlights contemporary poets with a substantial body of work to their credit; with this series we strive to resurrect work that has had limited distribution and is now out of print.

We are dedicated to giving all of the authors we publish the care their work deserves, making our catalog of titles the most diverse and distinguished it can be, and paying forward any earnings to fund more great books.

We've learned a few things about independent publishing over the years. We've also evolved a unique, resilient publishing model that allows us to focus mainly on vetting and preserving for posterity the most books of exceptional quality without becoming overwhelmed with bookkeeping and mailing, fundraising activities, or taxing editorial and production "bubbles." To find out more about what we are doing, come see us at www.futurecycle.org.

www.ingramcontent.com/pod-product-compliance
Lightning Source LLC
Chambersburg PA
CBHW060043050426
42448CB00012B/3115